I see the moon,

and the moon sees me....

To my mother Nell
remembering the days
when we read and sang these
rhymes together

I see the moon, and the moon sees me....

Helen Craig's book of Nursery Rhymes

Willa Perlman Books

An Imprint of HarperCollinsPublishers

Contents

Contents

Doctor Foster went to Gloucester
In a shower of rain;
He stepped in a puddle,
Right up to his middle,
And never went there again.

It's raining, it's pouring,
The old man is snoring;
He bumped his head
On the edge of the bed
And couldn't get up in the morning!

Teddy bear, Teddy bear, touch the ground,
Teddy bear, Teddy bear, turn around,
Teddy bear, Teddy bear, show your shoe,
Teddy bear, Teddy bear, that will do.
Teddy bear, Teddy bear, run upstairs,
Teddy bear, Teddy bear, say your prayers,
Teddy bear, Teddy bear, blow out the light,
Teddy bear, Teddy bear, say good night.

Wee Willie Winkie runs through the town,
Upstairs and downstairs in his nightgown,

Rapping at the windows, crying through the lock,
"Are the children all in bed, it's now eight o'clock."

I had a little nut tree, nothing would it bear
But a silver nutmeg and a golden pear;
The King of Spain's daughter came to visit me,
And all for the sake of my little nut tree.
I skipped over water, I danced over sea,
And all the birds in the air couldn't catch me.

Hickory, dickory, dock,
The mouse ran up the clock.
The clock struck one,
The mouse ran down,
Hickory, dickory, dock.

Dickery, dickery, dare,
The pig flew up in the air;
The man in brown
Soon brought him down,
Dickery, dickery, dare.

Mary had a little lamb,
  Its fleece was white as snow;
And everywhere that Mary went
  The lamb was sure to go.

It followed her to school one day,
  That was against the rule;
It made the children laugh and play
  To see a lamb at school.

There was an old woman who lived in a shoe,
She had so many children she didn't know what to do;
She gave them some broth without any bread
Then whipped them all soundly and sent them to bed.

16

© SIZE · 100 / GIANT

17

Bum, bum, bailey-O, two to one the barbel-O,
Barbel-O, barbel-O, bum, bum, bailey-O

Are you coming, Sir?
No, Sir. Why, Sir?
Because I've got a cold, Sir.
Where did you get the cold, Sir?
Up at the North Pole, Sir.
What were you doing there, Sir?
Catching polar bear, Sir.
How many did you catch, Sir?
One Sir, two Sir, three Sir.

House to let,
Apply within.
When you go out,
Somebody else comes in!

Ice cream, a penny a lump
The more you eat, the more you jump!
    Eeper Weeper. Chimney sweeper,
    Married a wife and could not keep her.
    Married another,
    Did not love her,
    Up the chimney he did shove her!

There was an old woman tossed up in a basket,
Seventeen times as high as the moon;
Where she was going I couldn't but ask it,
For in her hand she carried a broom.

"Old woman, old woman, old woman," quoth I,
"Where are you going to up so high?"
"To brush the cobwebs off the sky!"
"May I come with you?" "Aye, by and by."

One, two, three, four, five,
Once I caught a fish alive.
Six, seven, eight, nine, ten,
Then I let it go again.

Why did you let it go?
Because it bit my finger so.
Which finger did it bite?
The little finger on the right.

FEE! FI! FO! FUM!
I smell the blood of an Englishman:
Be he alive or be he dead,
I'll grind his bones to make my bread.

Jerry Hall,
He is so small,
A rat could eat him,
Hat and all.

Elsie Marley's grown so fine,
She won't get up to feed the swine,
But lies in bed till eight or nine.
Lazy Elsie Marley.

Jack be nimble
Jack be quick
Jack jump over the candlestick.

24

Little Boy Blue, come blow your horn,
The sheep's in the meadow, the cow's in the corn.
Where is the boy who looks after the sheep?
He's under a haycock fast asleep.
Will you wake him? No, not I,
For if I do, he's sure to cry.

To market, to market, to buy a fat pig,
Home again, home again, jiggety-jig.
To market, to market, to buy a fat hog,
Home again, home again, jiggety-jog.

Simple Simon met a pieman,
    Going to the fair;
Said Simple Simon to the pieman,
    Let me taste your ware.

Said the pieman unto Simon,
    Show me first your penny;
Said Simple Simon to the pieman,
    Indeed I have not any.

Simple Simon went a-fishing
    For to catch a whale;
But all the water he had got
    Was in his mother's pail.

Simple Simon went to look
    If plums grew on a thistle;
He pricked his fingers very much,
    Which made poor Simon whistle.

He went for water in a sieve
    But soon it all fell through;
And now poor Simple Simon
    Bids you all adieu.

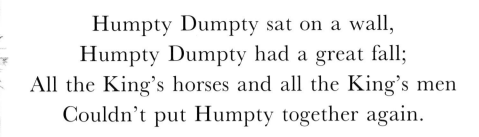

Humpty Dumpty sat on a wall,
Humpty Dumpty had a great fall;
All the King's horses and all the King's men
Couldn't put Humpty together again.

Pat-a-cake, pat-a-cake, baker's man,
Bake me a cake as fast as you can;
Pat it and prick it, and mark it with B,
Put it in the oven for Ben and me.

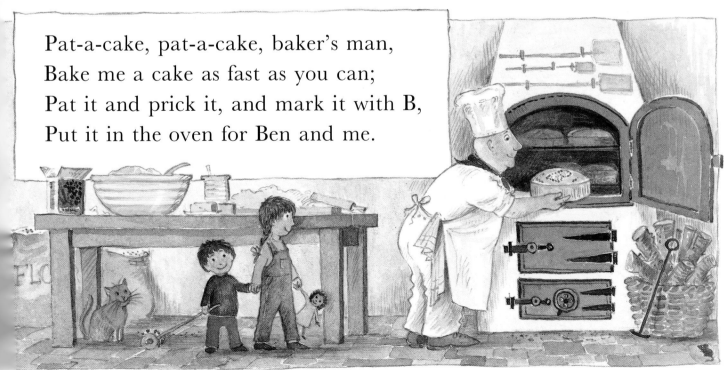

If all the world were paper,
And all the sea were ink,
If all the trees were bread and cheese,
What should we have to drink?

A wise old owl sat in an oak,
The more he heard the less he spoke;
The less he spoke the more he heard.
Why aren't we all like that wise old bird?

Three young rats with black felt hats,
Three young ducks with white straw flats,
Three young dogs with curling tails,
Three young cats with demi-veils,
Went out to walk with two young pigs
In satin vests and sorrel wigs;
But suddenly it chanced to rain
And so they all went home again.

Twinkle, twinkle, little star,
How I wonder what you are!

Up above the world so high,
Like a diamond in the sky.

Hey diddle, diddle,
The cat and the fiddle,
The cow jumped over the moon;
The little dog laughed
To see such fun,
And the dish ran away with the spoon.

There was a crooked man,
Who walked a crooked mile,
He found a crooked sixpence
Against a crooked stile.

He bought a crooked cat,
  Which caught a crooked mouse,
And they all lived together
  In a little crooked house.

A cat came fiddling out of a barn,
With a pair of bagpipes under her arm,
She could sing nothing but, Fiddle cum fee,
The mouse has married the humble-bee.
Pipe, cat; dance, mouse;
We'll have a wedding at our good house.

Little Poll parrot
Sat in his garret
Eating toast and tea;
A little brown mouse
Jumped into the house,
And stole it all away.

Six little mice sat down to spin;
Pussy passed by and she peeped in.
What are you doing, my little men?
Weaving coats for gentlemen.
Shall I come in and cut off your threads?
No, no, Mistress Pussy, you'd bite off our heads.
Oh, no, I'll not; I'll help you to spin.
That may be so, but you don't come in.

1, 2,
Buckle my shoe;

3, 4,
Knock at the door;

5, 6,
Pick up sticks;

7, 8,
Lay them straight;

9, 10,
A good fat hen;

11, 12,
Dig and delve;

13, 14,
Maids a-courting;

15, 16,
Maids a-kissing;

17, 18,
Maids a-waiting;

19, 20,
I've had plenty.

Hush-a-bye, baby, on the tree top,
When the wind blows the cradle will rock;
When the bough breaks the cradle will fall,
Down will come baby, cradle, and all.

Baa, baa, black sheep,
   Have you any wool?
Yes, Sir, yes, Sir,
   Three bags full;
One for the master,
   And one for the dame,
And one for the little boy
   Who lives down the lane.

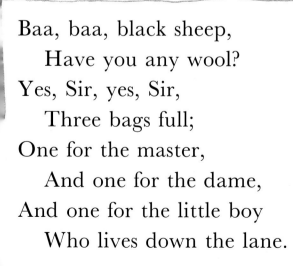

Jack and Jill went up the hill,
To fetch a pail of water;
Jack fell down, and broke his crown,
And Jill came tumbling after.

Then up Jack got, and home did trot,
As fast as he could caper;
He went to bed to mend his head
With vinegar and brown paper.

Four stiff-standers,
Four dilly-danders,
Two lookers,
Two crookers,
And a wig-wag.

?

There was an old woman
Lived under a hill;
And if she's not gone
She lives there still.

I do not like thee,
Doctor Fell,
The reason why
I cannot tell;
But this I know,
And know full well,
I do not like thee,
Doctor Fell.

Little Miss Muffet
Sat on a tuffet,
Eating her curds and whey;
There came a big spider,
Who sat down beside her
And frightened Miss Muffet away.

A man in the wilderness
asked this of me,
How many strawberries
grow in the sea.
I answered him,
as I thought good,
As many red herrings
as swim in the wood.

Mademoiselle
Went down to the well,
Combed her hair,
And brushed it well,
Then picked up her basket and
Vanished!

I see the moon,
    And the moon sees me;
God bless the moon,
    And God bless me.

Boys and girls come out to play,
The moon doth shine as bright as day.
Leave your supper and leave your sleep,
And join your playmates in the street.
Come with a whoop and come with a call,
Come with a good will or not at all.
Up the ladder and down the wall,
A half-penny loaf will serve us all;
You find the milk, and I'll find flour,
And we'll have a pudding in half an hour.

Gray goose and gander,
   Waft your wings together,
And carry the good king's daughter
   Over the one-strand river.

Three wise men of Gotham
Went to sea in a bowl;
If the bowl had been stronger,
My story would have been longer.

Incey Wincey spider
Climbed up the water spout;
Down came the rain
And washed poor Incey out;
Out came the sun
And dried up all the rain;
Incey Wincey spider
Climbed up the spout again.

Bat, bat, come under my hat,
And I'll give you a slice of bacon;
And when I bake,
I'll give you a cake,
If I am not mistaken.

Three blind mice,
  Three blind mice,
See how they run!
  See how they run!
They all ran after the farmer's wife,
  Who cut off their tails with a carving knife,
Did you ever see such a thing in your life,
  As three blind mice?

Oh the grand old Duke of York,
  He had ten thousand men;
He marched them up to the top of the hill,
  And he marched them down again.
And when they were up, they were up;
And when they were down, they were down.
But when they were only halfway up,
  They were neither up nor down.

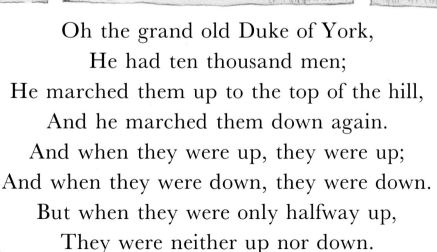

Goosey, goosey gander,
  Whither shall I wander?
Upstairs and downstairs
  And in my lady's chamber.
There I met an old man
  Who would not say his prayers;
So I took him by the left leg
  And threw him down the stairs.

Old King Cole
Was a merry old soul,
And a merry old soul was he;
He called for his pipe,
And he called for his bowl,
And he called for his fiddlers three.

Old Mother Hubbard
Went to the cupboard,
To fetch her poor dog a bone;
But when she got there
The cupboard was bare
And so the poor dog had none.

She went to the baker's
To buy him some bread;
But when she came back
The poor dog was dead.

She went to the undertaker's
To buy him a coffin;
But when she came back
The poor dog was laughing.

She went to the tavern
For white wine and red;
But when she came back
The dog stood on his head.

She went to the fruiterer's
To buy him some fruit;
But when she came back
He was playing the flute.

She went to the tailor's
   To buy him a coat;
But when she came back
   He was riding a goat.

She went to the hatter's
   To buy him a hat;
But when she came back
   He was feeding the cat.

She went to the cobbler's
   To buy him some shoes;
But when she came back
   He was reading the news.

She went to the hosier's
   To buy him some hose;
But when she came back
   He was dressed in his clothes.

The dame made a curtsy,
   The dog made a bow;
The dame said, "Your servant."
   The dog said, "Bow-wow."

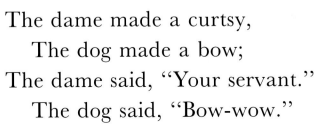

Library of Congress Cataloging-in-Publication Data
Craig, Helen.
   I see the moon, and the moon sees me . . . . : Helen Craig's book of
nursery rhymes.
        p.   cm.
   "Willa Perlman books."
   Summary: An illustrated collection of fifty-four nursery rhymes,
including "There Was a Crooked Man," "Hey Diddle, Diddle," and
"Bat, Bat, Come Under My Hat."
   ISBN 0-06-021453-8. — ISBN 0-06-021454-6 (lib. bdg.)
   1. Nursery rhymes. 2. Children's poetry. [1. Nursery rhymes.] I. Title.
PZ8.3.C8435Iaas   1993   92-18996
398.8—dc20   CIP
                                                     AC

Acknowledgments

Most of the nursery rhymes used in this book
are the versions I remember from my childhood;
a small selection have come from other sources
and these are gratefully acknowledged.

— *Helen Craig*

Jerry Hall, he is so small; *I see the moon*;
A wise old owl sat in an oak; *Little Poll parrot*; and
A cat came fiddling out of a barn are reprinted from
The Oxford Dictionary of Nursery Rhymes
edited by Iona and Peter Opie (1951)
by permission of Oxford University Press.
Bum, bum, bailey-O; *Are you coming, Sir?*; *House to let*;
Ice cream, a penny a lump; and *Mademoiselle went down to the well*
are reprinted from *Children's Games Throughout the Year* edited
by Leslie Daiken (1949) by permission of B. T. Batsford.

The End